GRAVITY

HELD TOGETHER BY GOD

A STUDY OF THE CHURCH FROM EPHESIANS

Gravity: Held Together by God
© 2017 by Jacob Abshire

Published by Truth411 and Lucid Books
18906 Par Two Cir., Humble, TX 77346
www.t411.com

Design and typeset: Resolute Creative Group, Inc., Houston, TX

Unless otherwise indicated, scripture quotations are from the ESV Bible® (The Holy Bible, English Standard Version®), copyright © 2001 by Crossway Bibles, a publishing ministry of Good News Publishers. Used by permission. All rights reserved.

GRAVITY

HELD TOGETHER BY GOD

t411.com

Truth411
HOUSTON, TX

LUCIDBOOKS

CONTENTS

Introduction 7

Lesson One: The Means of His Gravity 9

Lesson Two: The Aim of His Gravity 19

Lesson Three: The Model of His Gravity......................29

Lesson Four: The Source of His Gravity.......................39

Lesson Five: The Object of His Gravity.........................49

Lesson Six: The People of His Gravity 59

Lesson Seven: The Gifts of His Gravity 69

Lesson Eight: The Harmony of His Gravity.................79

Lesson Nine: The Result of His Gravity 89

Lesson Ten: The Effect of His Gravity 99

From the Author..109

Additional Resources 110

CONTENTS

INTRODUCTION

Think big. Think galaxy big. The observable universe is reported to have an estimated 200 billion galaxies or more. If our galaxy is anything like them, then they each have nearly 100 billion solar systems inside. Our system comprises eight unique planets that orbit around one large star, the sun. Each of these systems, big and small, are held together by an attractive force called *gravity*.

Now, think bigger. Think God big. "For by him all things were created, in heaven and on earth, visible and invisible, whether thrones or dominions or rulers or authorities—all things were created through him and for him" (Col. 1:15-16). He made all that stuff, as well as the stuff we haven't ventured out far enough to find yet. He made it all. Since it was made by Him and for Him, He has a vested interested in it all. So He keeps it alive. He keeps it moving. "And he is before all things, and in him all things hold together" (Col. 1:17).

Finally, think small. Think church small. It might not sound like a worthwhile idea, but there is a spiritual gravity at work in your community. God says the church is "joined and held together" by the power of God for the purpose of God's perfecting work (Eph. 4:16). As the sun, a galactic center, pulls stars and planets inward to maintain perfect order and rotation, so the Son pulls you and others inward to maintain a perfect order and function.

Where are you in God's cosmic system? Are you perfectly orbiting the Lord, contributing to His cosmic infinite purpose? Or, do you spend all of your energies trying to defy the attractive force of God's gravity?

> Rather, speaking the truth in love, we are to grow up in every way into him who is the head, into Christ, from whom the whole body, *joined and held together* by every joint with which it is equipped, when each part is working properly, makes the body grow so that it builds itself up in love. (Eph. 4:15-16)

Jesus prayed for unity just before His betrayal. He asked the Father to make all Christians one, just as He and the Father are one, in order to show the world that He was sent by the Father. The kind of oneness He desired was a spiritual result of salvation that would manifest in the church and to the world. God tells us, in the book of Ephesians, to "maintain the unity of the Spirit in the bond of peace" (Eph. 4:3). We are not to generate the unity, but preserve and keep it.

Following this, we are told how God uses His truth and power to effectively bring about practical unity in the church so the world would see it as the body of Christ and know that the Father sent the Son (Eph. 4:13-16). It is God answering the Lord's prayer.

If you are a Christ follower, you are a part of that answer. God is transforming you and the rest of the church into "one new man" (Eph. 2:15). This new man is Christ to the world. It is Christ as the head and the church as the body. Your part in this body is critical to its overall health.

In the following lessons, we will use Ephesians 4:15-16 to launch us into a progression of studies that focus on God's unifying work in the body by using the metaphor of gravity. The first five chapters will look at the subject from a high perspective, laying a foundation. They will focus on how the Lord unifies His body and to what purpose. The remaining chapters will dive deep into the subject to help you discover your place in the body in order to be used and experience the joy of fellowship.

The Father is answering the Son's prayer in the work He is performing in the church. You are a critical part to that answer. The life of the church and the mission of Christ depends on you and all who are in Christ. It's time to get into position and work your ministry.

THE MEANS
OF HIS GRAVITY

"speaking the truth in love"

While many scientific theories cannot be easily tested in our homes, gravity can. In fact, we test it every time we accidentally drop the television remote or our new smartphone. Gravity can be scary at times. It brings about bumps and bruises. It causes splatters and messes. But, it can also be incredibly wonderful. If we were not held to the ground by gravity, we would drift away into space.

Gravity is one of the most obvious forces at work in our universe, yet the greatest human minds have never been able to crack it. Scientists openly explain they know how gravity behaves, but know virtually nothing about what is. Truthfully, we may never know.

Gravity is defined as an unknown force of attraction that apparently exists between any two masses. It is everywhere—not just here on earth, but throughout all of the known universe. While scientists may lack answers about this force, Scripture reveals it is the power of God at work. For "in him all things hold together" (Col. 1:17), and "he upholds the universe by the word of his power" (Heb. 1:3).

In His providence, God has done the same for His church. According to Ephesians 4:15-16, Christ joins and holds us together for His sovereign purposes. In this series, we will unpack these two verses, word-by-word, to see God's mysterious force of attraction working in the life of His church. It is His divine gravity.

OPENING THOUGHTS

1. What are your most memorable experiences with gravity? Was it harmful to you or others or did you find it helpful and beneficial?

2. How does gravity influence our decisions each day? In what ways does gravity cause us to fear certain things and why?

THE INSTRUMENT OF TRUTH AND LOVE

Spiritually speaking, divine gravity is God's mysterious way of joining and holding together His church. More plainly, it is the power to unify. This is the primary emphasis of Ephesians 4:1-16. "Unity" is only used twice in the entire passage, but the concept is related in nearly every verse. We are urged to maintain unity by our actions (Eph. 4:1-3), instructed in the oneness of fellowship (Eph. 4:4-10), and encouraged by the work of cooperative training for like-mindedness (Eph. 4:11-14). The passage is clearly identifying God's force of attraction and what it means for us.

In our focus text, the first few words launch us into what might be described as the instrument of God's gravitational power. The apostle Paul, under the power of God, wrote about "speaking the truth in love" (Eph. 4:15). While few in words, the statement is vast in meaning.

First, "speaking the truth" is so basic and so crucial, the original language assumes it is actively happening among the church members. Every church of God is born and maintained by the gospel of Christ. It is built on the very "foundation of the apostles and prophets, Christ Jesus himself being the cornerstone" (Eph. 2:20).

Secondly, while we are speaking the truth, we are to do it in such a way that we are putting others before ourselves. Paul qualified our speaking with "in love" (Eph. 4:15). By this, he did not mean we are to romanticize the stories of the Bible, but to relate to each other in an attitude of humility, gentleness, and patience. It is the idea of *agape*, sacrificial love that assumes the weight of one another's burdens as our own (Eph. 4:2).

Read 2 Timothy 3:10-17 and answer the following questions.

3. In what ways do we speak the truth without love? How can we try to love by speaking the truth? Describe how these two go hand-in-hand.

4. Speaking the truth in love, according to the focus text, implies that we are needing to teach, reprove, and correct each other. What do you think these words mean? How are they done in love from a practical standpoint?

5. What does it mean that "all Scripture is breathed out by God"? What more does this teach us? How do you think continuing in God's truth relates to being joined and held together by God's power?

THE FUNCTION OF LOVE AND TRUTH

In Paul's first letter to Timothy, he said that "the aim of our charge (speaking the truth) is love that issues from a pure heart and a good conscience and a sincere faith" (1 Tim. 1:5). In other words, instruction is not the goal, love is. Instruction is the means to the goal. It is the instrument by which God brings about love between us, within us, and through us.

The writer of Hebrews put it this way: "Let us hold fast the confession of our hope without wavering … and let us consider how to stir up one another to love and good works … encouraging one another" (Heb. 10:23-25). The idea is that we should consider one another and encourage one another to stir up love. We do this by confessing our hope, or speaking the truth of God's Word.

At the same time, love seeks truth. Paul told the Corinthian believers that "love does not rejoice in wrongdoing, but rejoices with the truth" (1 Cor. 13:6). Love, according to the text, takes joy when truth is told. You can literally say that love loves truth. Evidently, the two hold hands wherever they may go. Love shapes the truth we speak and truth shapes the love we share.

Read 1 Corinthians 13:1-13 and answer the following questions.

6. What are some of the words that describe love? How are they evident when we speak or relate to each other in truth?

7. What does this passage say about the priority of love? Why do you think it is valued above all good and godly virtues? In what way do you think it contributes to God's gravity—joining and holding us together?

8. In hindsight, why do you think truth and love are of primary importance for God's gravity? What are some ways you can improve how you speak the truth in love?

CONCLUSION

The broader context of Ephesians 4 defines the truth by using synonyms like "the faith" and "the knowledge of the Son of God" (Eph. 4:13) as well as the "gospel" and "light" (Eph. 3:7-9). It is the entire counsel of God. And since God is love, it will always be accompanied by love (1 John 4:8). The two are not mutually exclusive concepts. God's gravity is at work when truth, dipped and saturated in love, is spoken to one another. How are your conversations? Do you speak truth to each other? Do you speak it in love? If not, then you are working against the gravity of God.

THE AIM
OF HIS GRAVITY

"we are to grow up "

You don't have to be a rocket scientist to know the importance of gravity. Without it, we would float away into cosmic darkness. Gravity holds the planets in a circular motion, without projecting them out like a slingshot. Gravity balances the small ligaments and fluid in our inner ear to help us walk. Gravity aids good bone growth and strong muscles, while at the same time reminding us that jumping high is an athletic feat. It has purpose and meaning. It is critical and necessary.

Still, we do all in our power to defy gravity. It's been in our bones since the early years of civilization. The Wright brothers literally broke ground with the first-of-its-kind, practical, fixed-wing aircraft. Their ingenuity made way for numerous other aircrafts to follow even today. The airline industry has made long-distance travel more efficient. With the advancement of shuttles and rockets, we can now lift ourselves into space and out of the sphere of the earth's gravitational power. We have, in a real sense, defied gravity, albeit with good intent.

In the same way, God's gravitational force—His power to join and hold together the church—is rich with purpose and meaning. It is in no way accidental or by coincidence. It has design, balance, intention, and effect. God's gravity glorifies Him and causes good for those who love Him. It brings order, harmony, and light.

At the same time, there are some who make every effort to defy the Lord's gravity, desiring to be loosed from His sovereign pull. There are some who belong near the "galactic center" and yet invent ways to lift themselves away. Sadly, there are even some who never enjoy the benefits of God's power because their desire for "space exploration" is constantly pulling them outside of God's will.

OPENING THOUGHTS

1. Why is it helpful to identify the purpose for something? How does design and intention bring meaning? How important is it to know why God joins and holds together His church?

2. How do order and harmony fit into God's design for the church? How does God's purpose relate to His gravity?

MATURED LIKE AN ADULT

With God, nothing is without purpose. "The Lord has made everything for its purpose," yes, "even the wicked for the day of trouble" (Prov. 16:4). This is an inescapable reality for a being who is both omnipotent and omniscient. You might say God can't help but do all things with purpose, even if it is simply to make Himself happy. But, in His inexhaustible wisdom, He infuses even the smallest of things with great purpose.

This was no foreign idea to Paul. He began his letter to Ephesus, as well as many others, by highlighting the sovereign purposes of

God: "Paul, an apostle of Christ Jesus by the will of God" (Eph. 1:1). God's perfect purposes were put together long before anything was made. He chose His church "before the foundation of the world" to be "holy and blameless before him" (Eph. 1:4). Paul used "predestined" to describe how God pieced together our existence. In doing so, He instills purpose. He designs us with a destination in mind. All things are according to God's purpose—His will, His end (Eph. 1:11).

The Lord is joining and holding us together for a very specific purpose. While we are "speaking the truth in love, we are to grow up in every way" (Eph. 4:15). Maturity is the purpose of God's gravity. When the instrument of truth and love is at work, the church is matured in every way. He likens it to the development of the human body. There is a time when it comes to its full age and competence. It is the peak of a person's life.

Read Ephesians 4:11-14 and answer the following questions.

3. In what ways did Paul describe the maturing of the church? How do these words and phrases contribute to your understanding of God's design for the church?

4. The phrase "mature manhood" is a reference to the perfection of a man's life—when his physical, emotional, and intellectual development are complete. How does this relate to the idea of "growing up in every way"? What new light does it shed on the maturing of the church?

5. How does truth fit into the perfecting of the metaphorical man in these verses? What evidences of the man's perfection can be observed?

BUILT LIKE A HOUSE

There is a more noticeable metaphor Paul used when describing the perfecting work of God's gravity. It is the concept of a building, one of Paul's favorite metaphors for the church. Earlier in the same letter, Paul employed this picture for good use:

> So then you are no longer strangers and aliens, but you are fellow citizens with the saints and members of the household of God, built on the foundation of the apostles and prophets, Christ Jesus himself being the cornerstone, in whom the whole structure, being joined together, grows into a holy temple in the Lord. In him you also are being built together into a dwelling place for God by the Spirit (Eph. 2:19-22).

Peter borrowed the same idea. He taught that the church was the building of God and that Christ was the "living stone" that was rejected by those not in the church (1 Peter 2:4). "You yourselves, like living stones are being built up as a spiritual house," which is to emphasize the idea of worship as Paul did, "to be a holy priesthood, to offer spiritual sacrifices acceptable to God through Jesus Christ" (1 Peter 2:5). Truth, saturated in love, creates a building agent that fortifies and structures a living community of God that is perfect and mature.

In ancient times, homes were not built of concrete and brick like they are today. They were built from the foundation up by stone—

one by another and on another. Each stone, when it is laid with the next, is reinforced to increase in strength and competence. Unlike today, aesthetics were of little consequence compared to the building's stability and resilience. This is the idea behind us being built up in every way.

Read 1 Corinthians 3:5-17 and answer the following questions.

6. When breaking up the quarrels of the Corinthian church, Paul had to remind them that all of God's leaders speak the truth in love for the same end. How did Paul describe the work of ministry and the foundation of the building?

7. Describe how the work of building is proven by stability and competence. How does the quality of the building material add to this idea? Why is it important?

8. How does knowing the purpose of God's gravity affect how you relate to others in the church? What are some practical ways you can bring this truth to life in your spheres of growth?

CONCLUSION

It is no coincidence that Jesus promised to build His church on the rock (or foundation) of the gospel—the good news of Himself (Matt. 16:18). There is nothing that will stop the Lord from finishing what He started. His power will eternally join and hold together His church until she is matured in every way. In our next lesson, we will look at the model of God's gravity and see what the fullness of maturity looks like for His church. Until then, consider how you might be a living stone in the building of God.

THE MODEL
OF HIS GRAVITY

"in every way into Him who is the head, into Christ"

In various social sciences, gravity models are used to describe certain behaviors that mimic gravitational interactions. For instance, one model communicates the decline of interaction between two locations when the distance is increased. In other words, a neighborhood that is nearer to a particular market will have far more interaction with that market than a neighborhood that is far away. (Yes, *scientists* figured this out.)

It is called a gravity model because the behavior of gravity illustrates the behavior of interaction between two points. The more distance between two objects, the less interaction they have. In these cases, gravity is used to bring simplicity to more complex concepts.

All models are meant to work this way. They simplify, clarify, and exemplify. They represent. They standardize. They demonstrate. Models bring light to something otherwise dimmed by unfamiliarity. They can also bring life to something that is otherwise desolate. Without models, some subjects are out of reach. We simply cannot grasp or picture them with information alone.

In most science classrooms, there is a small-scale replica of our solar system. Each planet is held in place by a thin metal pole that extends from a middle stem connected to the sun. It is designed to model what we are unable to see with our own eyes—namely, proportionate planets circling a large sun. No one assumes that this small plastic copy of the cosmos is the real system. No one looks at the sun, maybe three inches in diameter, and says, "Wow, the sun is smaller than I expected." Rather, we hold the model but grasp the big idea. We get a sense of the planetary system and are awestruck at its enormity and perfect harmony. Models serve this purpose.

OPENING THOUGHTS

1. Technically speaking, models are reproducible objects or people to be taken as an example. Who are some of the models in your life? What makes them a good example to copy?

2. Models also work as prototypes and even standards. How have you measured yourself by your examples? In what ways can you model God?

THE PREEMINENT PATTERN

Paul loved to talk about Christ. Addressing the church at Corinth, he said, "I, when I came to you, brothers, did not come proclaiming to you the testimony of God with lofty speech or wisdom," meaning fancy and persuasive words, "for I decided to know nothing among you except Jesus Christ and him crucified" (1 Cor. 2:1-2). Everything else mattered very little to him unless it was in tune with what Christ desired. To him, Christ was everything, and everything was for Christ.

You can see it all over his writings. In fact, he named "Christ" at least five times in the first three verses of Ephesians! Christ is authoritative and faithful (Eph. 1:1), gracious and peaceful (Eph. 1:2), blessed and heavenly (Eph. 1:3). Consider the remaining six chapters of the book. There are about 50 references to Jesus by name and nearly four times that including pronouns. The references to Christ in Ephesians outnumber its verses!

Read how Paul described Christ in his own words:

> He is the image of the invisible God, the firstborn of all creation. For by him all things were created, in heaven and on earth, visible and invisible, whether thrones or dominions or rulers or authorities—all things were created through him and for him. And he is before all things, and in him all things hold together. And he is the head of the body, the church. He is the beginning, the firstborn from the dead, that in everything he might be preeminent. For in him all the fullness of God was pleased to dwell, and through him to reconcile to himself all things, whether on earth or in heaven, making peace by the blood of his cross (Col. 1:15-20).

Paul was only making the obvious point. Christ is preeminent. He surpasses everyone and everything. He is the first, the greatest, the highest, the foremost. There is none more perfect, more distinguished, more honorable. All things were created through Him because there was no greater way. All things came after Him because there is no one before Him. He is the head because there is no one wiser, no one with more power, no one who has more authority. In Him dwells the fullness of God, and only in Him are all things reconciled.

There is no other way to measure perfection than to make Christ the standard. He is the picture of perfection, the model for maturity. While "speaking the truth in love, we are to grow up in every way *into him who is the head, into Christ*" (Eph. 4:15).

Read Romans 8:28-30 and answer the following questions.

3. According to this passage, to what purpose are we called as Christians? How would you describe all things working together?

4. How would you describe what it means to be "conformed to the image of his Son" to a new believer? Why would Jesus be called "the firstborn among many brothers"?

5. Explain the progression, a kind of cause and effect, described in verse 30. What is the connection between those who are predestined and those who are glorified? How does this relate to Christ being our head and standard?

THE PERSISTENT PERFECTION

Since Christ is our perfect picture, we are to be "imitators of God" and "walk in love as Christ loved us" (Eph. 5:1-2). Using "walk" to describe the way we live our life before God is suitable when we acknowledge that Christ is the "head of the church" (Eph. 5:23) and "we are his body" (Eph. 5:30). He takes the lead, and we do the walking. So, we should "walk in a manner worthy" of His name (Eph. 4:1).

This is why Paul urged us to do "as Christ" time and time again. We are to walk as Christ walked (Eph. 5:2), love as Christ loved (Eph. 5:25), lead as Christ led (Eph. 5:23), and care as Christ cared (Eph. 5:29). To put it in Jesus' words, "be perfect, as your heavenly Father is perfect" (Matt. 5:48).

There is a sense in which all who are in Christ are perfect already. "For by a single offering [Christ] has perfected for all time those who are being sanctified" (Heb. 10:14). This is a positional perfection. Because Christ is perfect, all who are in Him before God are also perfect. God applies the perfect life of Christ to us. Yet, we are still practically imperfect, which is why the writer of Hebrews described us as "being sanctified," or being made perfect. It carries the idea of completion and "the fullness of Christ" (Eph. 4:13). In other words, we "are being transformed into the same image from one degree of glory to another" (2 Cor. 3:18).

For every positional truth in Scripture, there is a corresponding practice to follow. For instance, we are spiritually alive (Eph. 2:4-5), but called to live the life (Phil. 1:21). We are made righteous (Rom. 1:17), but told to live righteously (1 John 3:7). We are children of God (Eph. 1:5), but need to act like God's children (1 Peter 1:14-15). We are cleansed (John 15:3), but must cleanse ourselves (2 Cor. 7:1). We are in Christ (Eph. 1:3), but make every effort to abide in Christ (1 John 2:28). The list goes on. Positionally speaking, we are perfect. Practically speaking, we need to be perfected.

Read John 17:20-26 and answer the following questions.

6. How does Jesus' prayer relate to God's gravitating work in the church? In what way does oneness contribute to and facilitate perfection?

7. "The glory that you have given me I have given to them." What do you think Jesus meant by this? How does it relate to us being made like Him?

8. How does this prayer bring you comfort today? What does it say about your spiritual growth and the work that God is doing in you?

CONCLUSION

Peter said that we will "become partakers of the divine nature" (2 Peter 1:4). The more God glorifies us in Christ, the more He is glorified. This is what Jesus meant when He said He has given us the glory that He received from the Father. It is the perfecting work of Christ joining and holding us together to be conformed into His image and likeness. We are growing up in every way into Him who is the head, into Christ. Picture Him. Imitate Him.

THE SOURCE
OF HIS GRAVITY

"from whom"

Physicists theorize that gravity is made up of tiny, unseen particles that emanate gravitational fields. They are called gravitons. Each bit pulls on every piece of matter in the universe. However, no one has ever found one. Modern science doesn't have the technology to see them, assuming they are actually there.

Einstein predicted gravitational waves over a century ago. In his theory of general relativity, these waves were basically ripples in spacetime generated by massive objects in the cosmos. Imagine a rock being dropped into a deep puddle of water and seeing the ripples emanate outward. In space, these waves are little particles of energy being carried away from the source. Since we can already measure waves, and waves are made up of particles, physicists believe if we can find a way to read these waves, we can find the gravitons.

Another theory, and a slightly more mystical one, revolves around the idea of "dark energy." The energy, or *ether* as some call it, is a substance at a quantum level that envelops and fills everything. It is sometimes considered to be a conduit for the life-giving force of the universe—sort of like midi-chlorians from the Star Wars space opera.

Other theories exist, but none have been able to provide any reasonable, concrete evidence in any direction. Gravity continues to elude the sharpest minds of humanity and most advanced technology we have created. Maybe one day we will discover the source of gravity. Or maybe not.

OPENING THOUGHTS

1. What do you think of when you consider the word source? Why do you think it is so critical to some that we find the wellspring of gravity?

2. The matter of source implies the question of origin and supply. Related to the church, what comes to mind when you think of origin and supply?

GOD'S UNLIMITED SUPPLY

We noted the preeminence of Christ in our prior lesson. He is supreme because of *who* He is and *what* He is. But, Christ is also supreme because of *when* He is—or more specifically, *when* He was. Speaking of God in terms of time is not easy. He is not bound by time. Rather, time is bound up in Him. He is "the Alpha and Omega," the beginning and the end, the one "who is and who was and who is to come" (Rev. 1:8). Before time existed, God existed.

This might be what Moses meant when he said, "in the beginning, God" (Gen. 1:1). It is certainly what the psalmist alluded in his stanza, "Before the mountains were brought forth, or ever you had formed the earth and the world, from everlasting to everlasting you are God" (Ps. 90:2). Of course, wrapped up in God's famous name, I AM, is the premise of an eternal being who has never changed, nor will ever change—ever. He is the same yesterday, today, and forevermore (Heb. 13:8).

By definition, this means that God is the source of everything that exists. Because He is limitless, He can remain the source of everything that exists, continually and forever. This is why Paul greeted the Ephesians with wishes of grace and peace "from God" (Eph. 1:2). The saints of the church are faithful "in Christ Jesus" (Eph. 1:1). Christians are described as being chosen "in him before the foundation of the world" (Eph. 1:4). Make no mistake, the prepositions "from" and "in," though small, carry a whole lot of power. They are like the gravitons of God's force.

These little bits are all over Ephesians. "In him we have redemption" (Eph. 1:7). "In him we have obtained an inheritance" of eternal life (Eph. 1:11). "In him" we are sealed with the promised Holy Spirit (Eph. 1:13). All good things are in Him because they are from Him. "Every good gift and every perfect gift is from above, coming down from the Father of lights, with whom there is no variation or shadow due to change" (James 1:17).

We are generators of nothing good. Even our faith to believe God came from Him (Eph. 2:8). Only the unchanging, eternal God can supply an unlimited amount of energy to maintain everything. This is where our focus text leads us. While "speaking the truth in love, we are to grow up in every way into him who is the head, into Christ, from whom" we are all joined and held together (Eph. 4:15-16).

Read Ephesians 3:14-21 and answer the following questions.

3. How might you interpret the phrase "according to the riches of his glory"? What did Paul mean when he used this phrase in connection to us being granted strength from God's power?

4. Why do we need to be strengthened by God's power? What is the role and purpose of Christ in this strength? What does love have to do with this?

5. What is meant by "filled" and "fullness" in verse 19? How does this fit within the bigger picture of the church and God's gravity?

GOD'S PROVISIONAL SUPPLY

God is the source of all things, even the purpose of all things. It is His right not only to assign purpose, but also to assume the authority to make sure all things meet the purpose He designed. It just comes with the territory. This is why Paul called Christ the "head" (Eph. 4:15). The head tells the body what to do. Christ's design for us is that we draw from His unlimited resources. He tells us to lean on His power, not our own.

The church in Galatia was guilty of trusting in their own energy. They were duped into thinking they could pull themselves up by their own bootstraps. Paul, writing a rather forceful letter to them, set them back on course. "Having begun by the Spirit, are you now being perfected by the flesh?" (Gal. 3:3). What God begins, He finishes (Phil. 1:6). The power that brought you into Christ will bring you all the way to heaven.

"Be strong in the Lord," Paul said (Eph. 6:10). We are to find strength in His strength, power in His power. We are to draw from His unlimited resources. For He "will supply every need of yours according to his riches in glory in Christ Jesus" (Phil. 4:19). We will never lack. God's storehouse will never empty. But we will empty, and we will need replenishing. For this reason, we are to draw from the spring of Christ. He is ever-flowing, and we must ever drink from His waters.

Read Ephesians 6:10-20 and answer the following questions.

6. Why do you think Paul connected the command to "be strong in the Lord and in the strength of his might" with the "whole armor of God"? What is being communicated to us?

7. Explain how the armor of God is used to wage war on sin and aid the work of being matured in Christ? What does each piece of the armor mean to you in light of God's joining and holding together His church?

8. Do you have a new appreciation for God's power? What can you do to assure yourself that you will continually drink from the fountain of Christ?

CONCLUSION

Charles Spurgeon said "prayer is the grandest power in the entire universe; that it has a more potent force than electricity, attraction, gravitation, or any other of those secret forces which men have called by names but which they do not understand."[1] He understood the key that unlocks God's power. Prayer is powerful because it is the yielding cry from a beggar who lives on the promises of God. And God, who has unlimited power, always performs His promises. This is why the whole armor of God should be accompanied by and put on through "all prayer and supplication" (Eph. 6:18).

God's power flows through His people as a life-giving force to join and hold us together in Him. Will you not seek His power?

---

[1] Charles H. Spurgeon (1834-1892), *True Prayer True Power*. Lulu Press, Inc, Aug. 26, 2014. books.google.com (april 1, 2017)

_____

_____

_____

_____

_____

_____

_____

_____

_____

_____

_____

_____

_____

_____

_____

_____

_____

_____

_____

_____

_____

_____

_____

_____

_____

_____

_____

_____

_____

THE OBJECT
OF HIS GRAVITY

"the whole body"

Our sun, a near perfect sphere of burning hot plasma, is the center of our solar system. It accounts for more than 99% of the entire system's mass. For perspective, it exceeds a quarter million times more mass than the earth. This means it has more gravitational power than any other object in the system. This is why eight known planets orbit it and not the other way around.

It is also the most important source of life for our planet. It keeps water and food sources in balance. It prevents the oceans from freezing over, stirs our atmosphere, and generates the weather patterns. The sun also gives energy to plant life, which turn around and provide oxygen and food. It helps us see, keeps us warm, strengthens our bones, and even lightens our mood.

The whole body of planets and stars in our solar system owe a great deal of honor to the sun. For if it were to increase mass, it would immediately throw everything into disarray. The earth would be sucked into its heat, burned up, and all life obliterated. If the sun were to lose a small bit of mass, the planets would fly off into the darkness, just after icing over and ruining all living things. Our system is a perfectly balanced stroke of genius by God (Gen. 1:16).

Similarly, God knitted the church together in such a way that it neatly works with its members to perfectly affect life within it. When there is an ideal harmony of truth and love, the divine gravity of God causes the waters to flow smoothly, the atmosphere to stir freshly, and the weather to stimulate vitality.

OPENING THOUGHTS

1. What is the church to you? What makes it? What defines it? How is it different from any other organized people group?

2. How would you describe a harmonious body of believers who are growing up in every way into Christ? What does it look like and why?

THE FORMATION OF THE BODY

The divine gravity Paul spoke about in our focus text is the spiritual power of God acting on "the whole body" (Eph. 4:16). He has chosen truth and love as His instrument, maturity as His aim, perfection as His model, and Christ as His source. He is working to "create in himself one new man," not many (Eph. 2:15). He is at work on the body as a whole—the body as one, the body as Christ, for it is the body *of* Christ.

This body transcends all places and all time. It was formed in eternity past, "before the foundation of the world" (Eph. 1:4). It was kept secret throughout all the Old Testament era, but revealed to the apostles and prophets in New Testament times (Eph. 3:3-5) as a unified figure made up of Jews and Gentiles alike. This is the "one new man" that God predestined according to His will (Eph. 1:5).

This is cause for celebration. The notion that we were adopted into the body before the world was created set Paul into praise mode. In the original language, Ephesians 1:3-14 is one long sentence of about 200 words. It is a song of worship from wonder to wonder. In it, Paul recognized a number of deep theological themes like election, sanctification, identification, adoption, redemption, inheritance, glorification, and more. He covers just about all fundamental doctrines of the body.

At the base of these doctrines is the reality of God's sovereign choice. Although it has been a matter of fierce debate, it is essential to our understanding and dramatically shapes the way we interpret our position and function in the body. The Word of Christ says that God "chose us" in eternity past (Eph. 1:4). This is also captured in the phrase "predestined us" (Eph. 1:5).

Divine election, as it is sometimes called, is found throughout Scripture, even in the Old Testament. Israel was elected (Ex. 6:7; Deut. 7:7-9). The angels were elected (1 Tim. 5:21). Christ was elected (1 Peter 2:6). Jesus made it clear to His disciples, "You did not choose me, but I chose you" (John 15:16). The church, and all who are in it, were also elected (2 Tim. 1:9; 2:10). "We ought to always give thanks to God for you, brothers beloved by the Lord, because God chose you as the firstfruits to be saved" (2 Thess. 2:13). Indeed, we ought to give thanks!

Read Romans 9:11-20 and answer the following questions.

3. How did Paul use the story of Jacob and Esau to communicate God's sovereign choice? Why did he include the phrase "they were not yet born and had done nothing either good or bad"?

4. Paul expected some to object to this teaching, so how did he respond, beginning with verse 14? How do God's mercy and compassion relate to His election?

5. Compare this passage with Ephesians 2:8-10. What do these scriptures teach us about our faith and the formation of the body of Christ?

THE ENTRANCE TO THE BODY

Election does not exclude human responsibility. People must still repent and believe in Christ. God calls us to respond in faith to the reality of the gospel. "All that the Father gives me will come to me, and whoever comes to me I will never cast out" (John 6:37). At the same time, Jesus said, "No one can come to me unless the Father who sent me draws him" (John 6:44).

These are two sides of the same coin. They are paradoxical, but not contradictory. We don't have to comprehend it, just apprehend it. God has it figured out, and we can trust Him to tie up loose ends that our minds can't wrap around. In fact, we can rejoice in the doctrine of election, for Paul said that God chose us "in love" (Eph. 1:4-5). There is nothing harsh about it. "In this is love, not that we have loved God but that he loved us" (1 John 4:10).

With that in mind, we can turn now to our response. The Father draws us to Him. He gives us to the Son. The Son casts out no one. According to Ephesians 2:8, it is by faith, which is given to us for salvation. In his gospel, John wrote, "But to all who did receive him, who believed in his name, he gave the right to become children of God, who were born, not of blood nor of the will of the flesh nor of the will of man, but of God" (John 1:12-13). How must we be saved? How can we enter into Christ and into His body?

Read Romans 10:8-13 and answer the following questions.

6. What do you think it means to "confess" and "believe"? How does this relate to your heart, will, and commitment?

7. Have you made the decision to come to Christ? If so, describe your experience and what it was like. If not, are you willing to make that decision now?

8. How does the reality of God's election shape the way we understand God's divine gravity? How does man's responsibility fit within that paradigm?

CONCLUSION

We know that anyone who desires to be saved will not be turned away. If you believe in what Christ has done for you, salvation is within your grasp. All you must do is confess and believe. "For everyone who calls on the name of the Lord will be saved" (Rom. 10:13).

The matter of divine choice and human responsibility is a suitable transition in our study series. We have been focusing primarily on God's corporate and structural work in the whole body. For the remainder of the series, we will focus on God's individual and functional work in the body's members. So, now that we understand the body, let's find our place in it.

THE PEOPLE
OF HIS GRAVITY

"by every joint"

Gravity holds the key to the surest way to weight loss. Since it is an attractive force between two bodies of mass, weight is proportionately measured. The closer you are to a large mass, such as the earth's surface or the ground, the heavier you become. So, the higher the altitude, the lighter the body. Objects farther away from the earth's center experience a decrease in the planet's gravitational pull. So, next time you are floating out to space, bring your scale. You'll be glad you did.

Gravity is relative to mass and distance. The bigger the mass, the heavier an object will be when it is nearer to another object with equal or greater mass. In reality, our mass would never change—only our distance to the power. The closer we are, the weightier we will become. Consequently, the farther we are, the lighter we will become. But, you will be sad to know, our mass will never change.

All masses in the universe have some kind of gravitational pull. So, when we are closer to the earth, we will feel the earth's gravity more. When we are closer to the moon, we will feel the moon pulling even more. If we were right in the center of two objects of greater mass than ours, we would be attracted by the one that is greater in mass. It's not difficult to understand. But, it does introduce a very weighty point—pun intended.

God is attracting us into Himself. His divine gravity is pulling and drawing us to Christ in order that we may be joined together and made perfect by His power. The closer we are to God and the longer we dwell in Him, the more mature we will become. The opposite is also true. The farther we are from God and the less we dwell in Him, the less we will be like Christ.

OPENING THOUGHTS

1. Biblically speaking, how can nearness to God affect transformation in us? What does God do to our life when we dwell together in His Son?

2. How does this reality play into the local assembly? What do church attendance, regular worship, and corporate fellowship have to do with God's maturing work in each of us individually?

WALK IN HIS FULLNESS

Over the past five lessons, we have been using Ephesians 4:15-16 to launch us into a series of studies on the church. We have learned that truth and love are God's instrument to mature His whole body with the intention of making it perfect by His power. This is the work of God's divine gravity. He is joining and holding together a people to form "one new man" (Eph. 2:15).

Now, we will turn our attention to the more personal aspect of the body and see how each of us fit within the larger work of God.

We will look at the people of the church. People like you. If you are in Christ, then you were once "separated from Christ, alienated from the commonwealth of Israel and strangers to the covenants of promise, having no hope and without God in the world" (Eph. 2:12). That is to say, we were all once far away from God's gravitational power. "But," Paul said, "now in Christ Jesus you who once were far off have been brought near by the blood of Christ" (Eph. 2:13).

When Jesus died on the cross, He effectually grabbed you out of the cosmos and brought you into His sphere of love. "For through him we both have access in one Spirit to the Father" and the hostility between us and God was abolished (Eph. 2:16, 18). So, we are "no longer strangers and aliens," but "fellow citizens with the saints and members of the household of God, built on the foundation of the apostles and prophets, Christ Jesus himself being the cornerstone, in whom the whole structure, being joined together, grows into a holy temple in the Lord" (Eph. 2:19-21).

No structure is finished until each of the stones has been laid. Christ is the cornerstone. We are the living stones that are laid by God together with Christ for the greatest purpose—to be a "dwelling place for God" (Eph. 2:22). There really is no higher calling. However, it does come with an expectation to walk in the fullness of Christ—near Him and in Him. If Christ is the head and we are the body, then we ought to walk like Him.

Read 1 John 1:1-4 and answer the following questions.

3. The church is a living community of God that is formed in the life of Christ. Follow the thoughts of John as he described the "life" and put it in your own words. What does this tell us about the members of the body of Christ?

4. What is the progression of fellowship in this passage? Explain why it is important for the body of Christ to keep in mind. How might it encourage you today?

5. According to verse 4, how might joy be made complete? How does this relate to the unifying work of God in the church?

ABIDE IN HIS LOVE

Before we were brought into Christ, we walked "dead in our trespasses and sins" and lived "in the passions of our flesh" as "children of wrath" (Eph. 2:1-3). But, God is rich in mercy. He "made us alive together with Christ" and prepared good works "that we should walk in them" from now on (Eph. 2:5, 10).

Our aim for the new life we now live is to be "imitators of God" and "walk in love" and truth, which is exactly what God uses to transform us (Eph. 5:1-2). So, "look carefully then how you walk, not as unwise but as wise, making the best use of the time because the days are evil" and because the life of the body depends on you (Eph. 5:15-16). Remember, it is the whole body that we are being joined into.

Perhaps, the best way to understand this worthy walk is in Paul's letter to Titus. He instructed the church to walk in a way "that in everything they may adorn the doctrine of God our Savior" (Tit.

2:10). Think of it as the suitable decoration on the gospel tree. It is the clothing of purity that dresses the truth of God's Word. It is that lifestyle that manifests all that Christ promises in Himself. If the gospel comes to make a man whole, then the man must walk in wholeness. If it comes to make a child obedient, then the child should act accordingly. This is the idea behind the new walk.

Spiritually speaking, we do this by drawing near to God. As the psalmist captured it, "For me, it is good to be near God" (Ps. 73:28). For when we are near Him, we are enveloped by His mercy and grace and empowered by the fellowship we have with the Son. It is the practice of being "filled with the Spirit" (Eph. 5:18). When we are filled, we walk in humility, gentleness, patience, bearing one another in love, maintaining unity in the bond of peace, grateful, having melodies in our heart, and submitting to each with gladness (Eph. 4:2-3; 5:19-21).

Jesus taught this. When establishing the basis of Christian living, He borrowed imagery from the agricultural world—vines and vine crops. He identified Himself as the true vine and the Father as the "vinedresser" or caretaker of the vine.

Read John 15:1-11 and answer the following questions.

6. What are the two types of vine branches and what do they teach us about the worthy walk? What is the difference between the two branches?

7. What does God do with the branches that are not fruitful? What does He do with those that are fruitful? How does this relate to being joined and held together by God's divine gravity?

8. Describe, in your own words, the walk of a person who abides in Christ. In your own assessment, are you making every effort to abide in Christ? If not, what do you plan to do?

CONCLUSION

The first step in the new walk is knowing that you are accountable to a whole body and it to you. Your part is vital. Your place is key. Your life is an important stone in the bigger building. God is maturing the church in every way, and He is doing it through you, "by every joint" and ligament and member. You belong to the body, and the body needs you to walk in His fullness. It relies on your fruitfulness. When you neglect your walk, the body feels it. Will you help the body? Will you abide in Christ by drawing near to Him and allowing God to work through you? Our next lesson will tell you how.

THE GIFTS
OF HIS GRAVITY

"with which it is equipped"

The sun has an unusually enormous amount of gravity. It uniquely pulls all of its own mass into a nearly perfect sphere. This is for good reason. The core of the sun is so hot, its temperatures and pressures create fusion reactions—homemade energy. The colossal quantities of light, pressure, and energy beaming from its core counterbalance its gravity and reach out into space for multiple light years.

The earth also benefits from gravity and contributes to life as we know it. Gravity holds together air pressure so we can breath. It does the same for plant life, which in turn feeds us oxygen. It is responsible for the rising and falling of tides. The moon, a much smaller mass than the earth, still has its fair share of gravity. As it rotates around the earth, its gravity causes the tides to rise.

At a more personal level, gravity helps our muscles, bones, and various others systems to function properly. All human movement is dependent on gravity. Progression itself, if you think about it, exists in a movement whereby the center of gravity is allowed to fall slightly in the direction of motion. Try walking without leaning.

If these masses were not infused with gravity, they would not function in a way that is suitable for life. Even human beings use gravity for the betterment of themselves and others. Being productive is a matter of learning and developing the tools to work effectively within gravity's power, and in some real way, by gravity's power.

OPENING THOUGHTS

1. When it comes to God's gravitational power at work in the church, how do you think we should function? How do we use His power to help each other?

2. If you are brought into God's system, the body of Christ, how are you to operate within it? How does God's gravity affect you personally and practically as it relates to your role in His church?

SPIRITUALLY, NOT SPONTANEOUSLY

In the past lesson, we introduced the idea that the body of Christ is made up of individual people. Each person was personally called by God and drawn into the body by the Holy Spirit. It is no accident, no coincidence, and it is not without purpose. We learned the purpose of our call, but what about the purpose of our function?

God joins and holds together the whole body "by every joint with which it is equipped" (Eph. 4:16). According to the text, the church is equipped *with* its members and *by* its members. Every member has been spiritually gifted to function in a specific way to contribute to the greater purpose. "But grace was given to each one of us according to the measure of Christ's gift" (Eph. 4:7).

This passage packs a lot within it. For starters, it tells us Christ has given us grace, which means "favor," and it is translated in other passages as "gift." It emphasizes a transaction that was undeserved. We did not earn God's grace. Rather, He gave it freely. He also gave it decisively. It was given "according to the measure." That is, He gave gifts as He desired, according to His purpose and will (Eph. 1:11), in different quantities and qualities. He also gave to "each one of us" so no one is left out. Every believer who was brought into the body of Christ has received a gift of grace by God.

This means that no one has excuse. No one is without. No one is insignificant. Everyone plays a vital role in the body of Christ. Some, like the leaders of the church, are gifted people given to the church as gifts. Ephesians 4:11-12 says these leaders are gifted at teaching and equipping the members to perform in their particular gift. In other words, they "equip the saints for the work of the ministry" (Eph. 4:12).

Spiritual gifts are the workings of the ministry. They are spiritual channels through which the Holy Spirit works to build up the body of Christ in a special way. They are not spiritual gifts because we are spiritual or qualified above others to receive them. They are spiritual gifts because they are spiritually given and spiritually worked.

Read 1 Corinthians 12:1-11 and answer the following questions.

3. Why is it important for us to be informed about spiritual gifts? What is the overall message of this passage as it relates to spiritual gifts?

4. How does it help us practically to know there are a variety of gifts but one Spirit who works each of them? Describe the gifts included in this cursory list.

5. What is significant about verse 11? What does it teach you personally and how does it motivate you to do the work of ministry?

UNITY, NOT UNIFORMITY

Each of us are gifted to maintain the unity of the faith. But, we are not all gifted the same. For God "apportions to each one individually as he wills" (1 Cor. 12:11). He gives different gifts to different people. Different people with similar gifts have been gifted to use their gifts differently.

The body is designed to have unity, not uniformity. It is not for us to put each gift in a box with a label on it, but to understand that each of us has a blended measure of a variety of graces that together make our gift unique to us. For instance, several people might be gifted to teach. But, they are not all gifted to teach in the same way or with the same measure. One might teach one way with more mercies, while another in a different way with more technicality.

It is not that everyone with the gift of leadership leads the same way. Nor is it that everyone with the gift of giving gives the same way.

Rather, everyone is unique, and everyone is vital. Each member functions in a way that no one else can function. If there were two who did the exact same thing, one would be redundant. But God made everyone in the body critical.

The implications are huge. We are to "work together with him" and not "receive the grace of God in vain" (2 Cor. 6:1). In other words, don't waste your gift. Don't flounder the power God put inside you. Find it. Work it. Use it. And the body will grow.

Read Romans 12:3-8 and 1 Peter 4:10-11, and answer the following questions.

6. Why should we not think of ourselves "more highly than [we] ought to think"? What does this have to do with "the measure of faith that God has assigned" us?

7. What did Peter tell us to do with our gifts? How are we to do it? Why did he include "by the strength that God supplies"?

8. What does all of this mean for you today? How might your life in Christ look differently going forward? What sort of changes will you make, if any?

CONCLUSION

There is no greater reward on earth than to be plugged into the body and helping it grow by functioning in the gifted role God designed for you. When you do, everything is wonderful. Everything is exciting. Everything works for God's glory. Even when you face challenges, you are pleasantly filled with joy.

If you want to experience this joy, but don't know what your spiritual gift is, here are some practical steps to find it. First, pray and ask God to make it known (James 1:5). Second, yield yourself to Christ (Rom. 6:13). Third, be continually filled with the Spirit (Eph. 5:18). Fourth, walk in the Spirit (Gal. 5:16). Fifth, serve with others and observe. God's Spirit shines when we serve and submit to each other in the church. He will protect the church from your mistakes and guide you toward the specific function He has set aside for you. Once you've discovered your gift, seek to continually develop it for God's glory and the work of ministry.

THE HARMONY
OF HIS GRAVITY

"when each part is working properly"

From a good distance away, it would appear as a unified source of light. In actuality, our solar system is a wonderful blend of unique planets orbiting a single star. Each planet is distinct from its siblings. They are all different sizes, different colors, and different distances from the same sun. While all planets rotate and orbit, none of them rotates on the same axis. This means that a full rotation (what we would call a "day" period) is also unique.

We experience a 24-hour day. So does Mars, give or take an hour. But Jupiter, Saturn, Uranus, and Neptune all have shorter days. Jupiter rotates in only 10 hours and Saturn in 11. Both Mercury and Venus take the trophy for lengthy days. Venus has a whopping 5,808 hours in a full day (242 of our days).

The same is true of a full orbit. We measure a full orbit around the sun as 365 days. Mars orbits in half the speed. If you lived on Mars, there would be 687 days per year. Neptune, the farthest planet from the sun, would experience 165 of our years in one trip around the sun. Mercury, the nearest to the sun, does it in only 88 days.

If these numbers tell you anything, it is that our single planetary body is made up of many different members. Their distinctions run deep. Some are gas planets. Some are solid. Some have multiple moons. Some have none. They each have unique temperatures, seasons, atmospheres, chemical balances, and more. However, they all manage to maintain a harmonious system of planetary balance. No planet interferes with another and causes disorder. It is a body of peace.

This is how God designed the church. It is a single body of Christ followers who are "eager to maintain the unity of the Spirit in the bond of peace" (Eph. 4:3). Although each member of the body is critical, no two members are alike. God has gifted them each in their own way. But, when "each part is working properly," the fullness of Christ is made manifest (Eph. 4:16).

OPENING THOUGHTS

1. How do you notice or identify the uniqueness of each member in the church? In what ways are we different from each other?

2. How can our differences become problems? How might our differences bring about more unity? When have our differences been a challenge?

THE REALITY OF ONENESS

While it is true that God, in His limitless wisdom, knows exactly what the body needs to grow up into the fullness of Christ, it doesn't mean that there won't be any challenges. Not every member will be spiritually minded at all times. We can, as Paul said, "quench the

Spirit" (1 Thess. 5:19). This means we can let ourselves get in the way of God's work.

The Spirit builds up the body through the channels of our gifts. It is possible, when we are not focused on truth and love, to spiritually "clog" the channel, preventing the power to flow. Timothy, the protege of the apostle Paul, was guilty of this. Paul urged him in two different letters to "not neglect the gift" he had, but to fan it into flame (1 Tim. 4:14; 2 Tim. 1:6). This is an easy trap to fall into.

Another way we can quench the spirit is by neglecting the assembly. The writer of Hebrews urged us to "consider how to stir up one another to love and good works, not neglecting to meet together" (Heb. 10:24-25). In other words, God cannot use you to build others up if you are not assembling with the body. Quenching the spirit happens when we neglect the gift and neglect the gathering.

Neglect is failing to look after something. It refers to disregard and mishandling. The church in Corinth was full of the gifts and full in their assembly. But, they were still neglecting both. The church was largely divided by its members' ability to show off spiritually. Some who claimed to have the more spectacular gifts were considered to be more spiritual. The remaining members, gifted in less celebrated ways, were seen as unspiritual.

To add to that, they fought over heroes. Some said, "I follow Paul." Others said, "I follow Apollos." Still yet, others claimed Cephas. The really pious ones took the high road and said, "Well, I follow Christ" (1 Cor. 1:12). But Paul threw it back in their faces and asked them all, "Is Christ divided? Was Paul crucified for you? Or were you baptized in the name of Paul?" (1 Cor. 1:13). Of course not. The Corinthians lost sight of the true nature of the church. It belongs to God, for it is the body of Christ.

Read 1 Corinthians 12:12-20 and answer the following questions.

3. How did Paul establish the concept of real diversity in the church? Who belongs to the body? How does everyone get into it?

4. Explain the illustration of the body parts. What does it tell us about the reality of the church and the importance of its members? What does it say about the value of each member?

5. According to the passage, how are we to treat others with gifts that are different, possibly less noticeable? What role should honor and modesty have among the members of the church?

THE INTENTION OF ONENESS

Salvation is the entrance into the body. It is also the initial point of unity. All Christians are one. Spiritual baptism is God placing a new believer into the body of Christ. "For in one Spirit we were all baptized into one body" (1 Cor. 12:13). It happens the moment we repent and believe. Immediately, the believer is grafted into the body. "In him you also, when you heard the word of truth, the gospel of your salvation, and believed in him, were sealed with the promised Holy Spirit" (Eph. 1:13).

Every believer is in the body of Christ, and the Spirit of Christ is dwelling in them. "Anyone who does not have the Spirit of Christ does not belong to him" (Rom. 8:9). There is no such thing as a Christian without the Spirit. Nor is there such a thing as a Christian who does not belong to the body. This is why we are told to "*maintain* the unity of the Spirit" (Eph. 4:3). The unity is already there. We only need to look after it, not neglect it.

On the other hand, we are told to "*attain* to the unity of the faith" (Eph. 4:13). This is different. It is not a reality, but a goal. In one sense, our unity has been accomplished through Christ. In another sense, our unity needs to be lived out and brought to manifest in the life of the church.

According to our next focus passage, unity in the body is accomplished by walking in a selfless manner. It is taking the truths of Scripture and allowing yourself to be washed in love. Paul described it as being a prisoner for the Lord, and thereby the Lord's body.

Read Ephesians 4:1-6 and answer the following questions.

6. Explain the words and phrases Paul used in verse 2 to describe the manner of our walk. Give examples of these in action within the life of the church.

7. Why do you suppose Paul used "maintain" when speaking about our contribution to the unit of the body? How might we "maintain the unity"? What is the "bond of peace," in your opinion?

8. What are some practical ways for you to promote unity among the church? What things can you do, or not do, to ensure others feel knitted into the body?

CONCLUSION

Oneness with each other is an important matter. Without exception, every biblical image of the church lays stress on unity. It is the crux of God's gravity and the key to turning the world right-side up. The question for you today is, what will you do with the unity you have with Christ and His body? How will you seek to maintain the reality of oneness and the intention of oneness? In our next lesson, we will look at what happens when oneness is sought and, in some respects, found.

THE RESULT
OF HIS GRAVITY

"makes the body grow so that it builds itself up"

Over the last eight lessons, we have used gravity as a springboard to study God's divine work in His body. From the mysteriousness of its power to the delicacies of its effects, gravity has helped us join together our thoughts with God's truth. In a way, it has been used as God designed it—for His glory.

Gravity glorifies God as we study and discuss its many conundrums. It glorifies God when we reach our limits and acknowledge that God is much more versed with His creation than we are. Gravity reminds us that God is far bigger than we can imagine and far more intelligent than we would ever credit Him. Gravity reveals, in a big way, God so cares for all of us, that He designed this vast "garden" over which He has also given us dominion. It also informs us of how small the details are and the great length to which God went to make everything. Gravity points us far beyond ourselves to wonder about the God of creation.

It has also glorified God in helping us understand rich truths about His supernatural design for His supernatural body. When we briefly take our eyes off the dark sky and lay hold of the gift of God's church, we are thrilled all over again. All of the power and wisdom that are behind the making of the cosmos are also behind the making of the church. All of the creativity and purpose poured into the galaxies was also poured into the community of God. What a tremendous thought!

Gravity does, however, have its limits, as we will see in this lesson. While it does help sustain life on earth, it does not enable it to produce any. Gravity has no power to make the solar system better. It only *maintains* what exists. It can do no more. But God's church, when His power is at work in it, can do far more.

OPENING THOUGHTS

1. How is God's power, that joins and holds His church together, different from the force that holds masses in balance? Why is His work unique in the church?

2. What do you think God intends to do with the church as His power works in it? How will the church look and function when it is brought to its fullness?

A DEVOTED BODY

Our study has brought us through many things. We first looked at the instrument of God's gravity. It is the truth. And by its very nature, being the truth of God, it is also love. The two are inseparable. These two make up the means by which the body of Christ is built up. The standard, or blueprint for the building, is none other than Christ, who is also the source and authority of the body. He works, through the power of the Holy Spirit, to bring transformation to the whole body of believers. This is what we are calling God's gravitational force—bringing together His people to form one body through which He dwells in the earth.

We then turned our focus to the body's members. We are the individuals He transforms and renews into mature people of faith and knowledge. To be clear, the work God performs is a work of renewal that taps the mind in order to shape the heart (Rom. 12:2). It is the transformation from the inside out. He does this through gifted leaders who equip the members to perform their ministries to which they were personally called. When these ministries function by the power of God's Spirit, they produce maturity in the other members and bring about invincible unity. Where there is no maturity, there will be no unity.

In our final two lessons, we will see how all of this comes together. In short, it will result in a body that is equipped to withstand being "carried about by every wind of doctrine, by human cunning, by craftiness in deceitful schemes" (Eph. 4:14). Furthermore, it will bring about a perfect love that makes Christ famous throughout the world. In this lesson, we will focus on the initial result—how each member "makes the body grow so that it builds itself up" (Eph. 4:16).

Acts 2 describes the very first church of God. It is a dynamic story. After Jesus resurrected from the dead and ascended into heaven, the disciples were praying in an upper room. Then, a sudden sound and rushing wind swept in and filled the room. The Holy Spirit came into each of them, and they immediately proclaimed God's wonders in unlearned, foreign languages. Crowds outside were astonished and asking questions. Peter saw it as an opportunity to preach the gospel. The crowd was "cut to the heart" and begged to be saved (Acts 2:37). That day, the church went from 120 to over 3,000 members with just one sermon, and the first church was born.

Read Acts 2:41-47 and answer the following questions.

3. What did the new church devote themselves to, according Acts 2:42? What does it mean to devote yourself to something? Describe a person's devotion in action.

4. What happened when they devoted themselves to these things? How did God move within their body and in the communities around them?

5. Describe the spirit of the people and how they were drawn to each other. What things did they do to maintain the unity of the Spirit and attain the unity of the faith?

A HEALTHY BODY

The explosive story of the first church gets better and better. After that big day, there were bigger days. Just two chapters later, the disciples were continuing in their devotions, and God added to their numbers. "Many of those who had heard the word believed, and the number of the men came to about five thousand" (Acts 4:4). In ancient writings, these numbers generally referred to the men, not the women and children. So the numbers could easily have been 20,000 by that day.

It didn't stop there. A short time later, the Jewish officials were filled with rage and sought to stop the Christian movement. They killed Stephen as he proclaimed the gospel, but this only fueled the fire of the church. "The word of God continued to increase, and the number of the disciples multiplied greatly in Jerusalem" and even "many of the priests" were saved (Acts 6:7). By then, the numbers were too large. The author couldn't keep count. Still, it didn't stop there. "So the church throughout all Judea and Galilee and Samaria had peace and was being built up," that is, the church was building itself up (Acts 9:31). By this point, the author had given up on keeping track of the church's size. He simply said "it multiplied" (Acts 9:31).

When the members of the church reach maturity, it becomes what you can call a "healthy" body. It is not that every member is without sin, not even that any member is without sin, but that the members are working together, devoted to the Lord, building the body up. You can see it first with the leadership. Remember that God gave gifted men to the church "to equip the saints for the work of the ministry" (Eph. 4:12). They are the *equipped ones* God uses to equip others.

It starts with the pastors. But when the leadership is lugging the load by themselves, the church is not healthy. So it is also seen in its members. The members are the ones working the ministry, participating in the life of the church and meeting the needs of one another. It is seen in strong discipleship, passionate worship, consistent prayer, deep fellowship, giving, and evangelism. In short, a healthy church is a wellspring for other churches. It doesn't reach out *for* help, but reaches out *to* help. It is a body that plants churches and trains churches. It reproduces itself. It is a church where God's gravity is evident and strong.

Read Matthew 16:13-20 and answer the following questions.

6. Explain what Jesus meant by "on this rock I will build my church" (Matt. 16:18). How does this relate to our series on God's gravity?

7. What happens when God builds His church? How does this bring all of the lessons together? What sort of power does God give to His church when it is matured by His Spirit?

8. How has this lesson changed or affirmed your thoughts about the church? How does it motivate you to participate in the life of the church as a member?

CONCLUSION

When the church devotes herself to the Lord, the Lord devotes Himself to the church. This is His desire. In Ephesians 5, we find what Paul referred to as a profound mystery. It is how the picture of marriage teaches us about the love of Christ. "Husbands," he said, "love your wives, as Christ loved the church and gave himself up for her, that he might sanctify her, having cleansed her by the washing of water with the word, so that he might present the church to himself in splendor, without spot or wrinkle or any such thing, that she might be holy and without blemish" (Eph. 5:25-27). This is the gravity of God illustrated by marriage. God "nourishes and cherishes" the body so that it becomes mature, lacking in nothing, but is also a wellspring of grace to others.

THE EFFECT OF HIS GRAVITY

"in love"

Gravity, and its many mysterious characteristics, has helped us during this series to grab hold of divine truths about God's church. When considering the bigger picture of our universe, we can easily be awestruck with the wonders of God's creativity and ingenuity. We can see His handiwork all over the universe, from the stars to the planets to the vastness of empty space.

God has so intricately designed the cosmos for His glory. Its complexities will never be exhausted by our technology or science. It is beyond our reach. And yet, it is right outside our window. We can see it from our home and study it with our telescopes. It is a gift from God that points us toward Him.

There is another gift of God that points us toward Him. It is the body of Christ. The church was designed to be a wondrous picture of Christ so that the world may look upon us and be drawn to the gospel that we proclaim. We are a living system of members, uniquely and skillfully made to work the ministry, as the Lord "joins and holds us together" to build us up into Christ.

OPENING THOUGHTS

1. How do you think the church fits into the bigger plan of God's glory? Practically speaking, how does your church fit into that plan?

2. What have you learned about God's gravitational work in the church so far? What truths have stood out the most?

LOVE AND PURITY FOR THE SAKE OF THE BODY

Our study will now come full circle. We began looking at the instrument of God's gravitational power—the word of truth spoken in love. Truth has been with us the entire way. It was the truth that brought us into the body (Eph. 1:13). Speaking the truth to each other is part of dwelling in the body because it infuses life into it (Eph. 4:15; 4:25). It also cleanses the body from sin (Eph. 5:26). Truth is the life-power flowing through the body like blood, fueling its growth and pumping its heart.

When truth is spoken in love, God's power permeates and accomplishes His will in the church, rooting and grounding it in love (Eph. 3:17). It matures the church, transforming its members into a fully furnished, functioning community. It is, from beginning to end, a work of love. For it was "in love" that God predestined us to be adopted as sons (Eph. 1:4). It was by His love that we received faith and were saved (Eph. 2:4). It is "in love" that we experience true unity (Eph. 4:2). It is "in love" that the church builds itself up (Eph. 4:16).

This is why we are told to be imitators of God as His "beloved children" and to "walk in love as Christ loved us" (Eph. 5:1-2). It is "in love" that we are to relate to our spouses, family, and community (Eph. 5:22-33). God's incorruptible love is to flow through the life of the church, inside and out, beginning and end.

Read Ephesians 5:1-20 and answer the following questions.

3. What is the connection between being "imitators of God" and being "beloved children"? How has God shown His love to us? How does He continue to show His love to us?

4. Paul told us to "walk in love" and then spent most of his words relating how we are to be pure and holy. What do you suppose this means? Can we walk in love without purity?

5. The close of this passage deals with mutual submission. Give illustrations of this submission in action in the church. How does it show love? Finally, how does holy living relate to all of this?

LOVE AND UNITY FOR THE SAKE OF THE WORLD

Since creation, God has desired to communicate His truth to humanity. After the fall in Eden, He used Israel as His primary vehicle. They were set apart to live in such a way that showed the world the perfect qualities of God. In the fullness of time, God sent His Son into the world to be His primary vehicle of truth to the world. Jesus was "the radiance of the glory of God and the exact imprint of his nature" (Heb. 1:3). This was the crowning mark of God's communication of truth. Jesus represented and proclaimed God's truth with complete accuracy. He was the perfect Word of God.

When Jesus ascended into heaven, He promised to send His Holy Spirit as a "Helper, to be with you forever, even the Spirit of truth" (John 14:15-17). In Acts 2, we see this promise fulfilled. The Spirit of Christ came down to the earth to indwell the hearts of believers and has been indwelling our hearts ever since. Now, the church is God's primary vehicle by which the Lord communicates His truth to the world. This is what it means to be the body of Christ. For in His absence, we are carrying on His mission of proclaiming and exemplifying the Word of truth. This is why our Lord commands us to "be perfect, as your heavenly Father is perfect" (Matt. 5:48). Jesus was perfect while He was here. Now, we are to be perfect as we are here.

When describing perfection, we have put emphasis on only one side of the definition—to be holy and whole, lacking in nothing. But Paul used the word in Ephesians to also refer to the bringing together of dislocated ligaments. When used in reference to a body, it refers to a kind of surgery by which the body parts are grafted and knitted in as they should be. Of course, this is the idea of unity, being made whole as a body. It is the concept behind gravity and the focus of our series.

When the body of Christ is perfect, unified and whole, the perfect qualities of God are communicated to the world. Jesus was God's exact imprint. He manifested God's love, holiness, wisdom, power, and authority in its truest sense because He is God. Being whole as a church is being one body representing these qualities to the world in Christ's stead. So, when the church is most whole, the gospel is most bright.

Read John 13:31-35 and answer the following questions.

6. The words "one another" do not refer to just any people in our sphere. Rather, they refer to "mutual others." What do you suppose this means? What is Jesus telling His disciples here?

7. How can loving "mutual others" tell people that we belong to the body of Christ? Why is this such a strong command from Jesus to us today?

8. Summarize the emphasis of the entire series in your own words. How has it made you more confident in God's work among the community of faith? What insights have you gained and how might life be different for you going forth?

CONCLUSION

All of this might sound like too much. Unity is difficult when people are challenging. Love is taxing when it is not reciprocated. Speaking truth is grueling when it so often conflicts with culture. But Paul gave us this praise:

> Now to him who is able to do far more abundantly than all that we ask or think, according to the power at work within us, to him be the glory in the church and in Christ Jesus throughout all generations, forever and ever. Amen (Eph. 3:20-21).

Confidence belongs to us because we belong to Christ. He is able. He can finish what He started. After all, it is His glory on the line, and He will not fail Himself. Paul's good-bye is a fitting way for us to close on the supremacy of God's love:

> Peace be to the brothers, and love with faith, from God the Father and the Lord Jesus Christ. Grace be with all who love our Lord Jesus Christ with love incorruptible (Eph. 6:23-24).

JACOB ABSHIRE

Hi. My name is Jacob Abshire and I am desperate for Jesus Christ. He is my way, truth, and life. My wife agrees—for herself, that is. She is equally desperate. Together, we love to call Him ours.

We also love to raise our four children to call on Jesus the same way. We live in Houston—the greatest "country" in the United States. We love to worship with our spiritual family at Northeast Houston Baptist Church.

My joy in life is to use creative means to bring others closer to God's word in order to find the riches of God's truth for the glory of God's son. In other words, I am "creatively making disciples." One of the ways I do this is by writing. First, I write at my personal blog (jacobabshire.com) where I turn up writings about church and family life, ministry, leadership, technology, scripture, and general musings. Second, I write books (because my friends pressure me to). In 2009, I published *Forgiveness: A Commentary on Philemon*. Three years later, I followed it up with *Faith: A Commentary on James*. Both are part of an ongoing series I call, "Reader's Commentaries," because they are comprehensive commentaries in a readable form. (One reader said that they are for people who hate to read but want to learn the Bible.) I also write small group discussion guides and design artwork consistent with my joy (all of which are available on my site).

For more information, visit my blog. If you have questions, shoot me a message on my contact page. I usually respond the same day. Grace and peace.

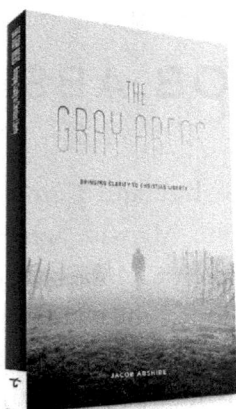

THE GRAY AREAS

BRINGING CLARITY TO CHRISTIAN LIBERTY

Nothing destroys a Christian relationship like a cold beer. It's happened a thousand times. Two were once good friends, and both saw the other as walking so close to heaven, they carried the mist from celestial clouds. But then, one saw the other in a restaurant with a cold glass of fizz, and heaven fell down. Why? Because spiritual people don't drink beer. Or watch movies. Or eat in pubs. Or smoke cigars. Or … fill in the blank.

We all know those things certain Christians call evil and others call good. They range from pant lengths to pew colors. They can be almost anything. And these things raise just as many questions about whether they are right or wrong. If you like to knock down a cold one or feel like R-rated movies are not for Christians, this book will help.

The Gray Areas was written to facilitate group discussion on making godly decisions when right and wrong are not so evident. The lessons will get under your skin and force you to think more deeply about your choices. Additionally, it will help you think more biblically about church community and enjoying life in light of those around you.

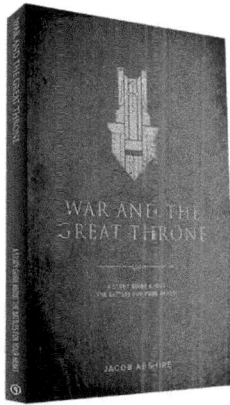

WAR AND THE GREAT THRONE

A STUDY GUIDE ABOUT THE BATTLES FOR YOUR HEART

The Bible uses the word "heart" to describe the inner you—the critical part of your existence, the part that lives forever. It is where your intellect and will shake hands, make friends and make moves. It is the part of you that is you. It the seat of your soul. And, it is exactly what we are discussing in this series. The "throne" is used metaphorically to refer to your heart. And, pressing the metaphor further, we will bring in some elements of medieval war that serves as illustrations of our fight against sin, the sufferings we endure, the weapons of war, and the people who support and hold us up in battle.

Each chapter, including the introduction and closing, tells as complete story with you as the main actor. So journey through the story of the *War and the Great Throne*. Get caught up in the story and most importantly, let the King, who has established His throne in the heavens and rules over all, search your heart and help you wage your war against the enemy of your soul.

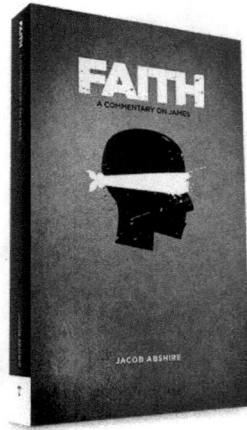

FAITH

A COMMENTARY ON JAMES

Do your troubles reveal faith that can save? In the Bible, James progresses through a series of troubles like the ones you face and ones you may not even know you face. He calls them trials. When our sinful lives collide against the holiness of God and our pride is smashed to pieces, we find the foremost gift of God as deposited in us by Christ. In our wreckage, we can learn to appreciate our troubles for what they are—divinely purposed trials that reveal and mature our belief in Christ. In this book, we will follow along with James and see what we can uncover about the foremost gift of God: Faith.

Find out why trials are our greatest gifts … This book explores 18 characteristics of faith in order to help you mature as a Christ follower. But before you can begin your journey, you must be ready and willing to let the waves wreck you again and again.

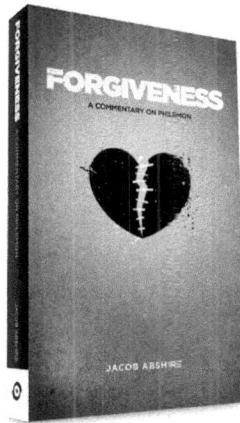

FORGIVENESS

A COMMENTARY ON PHILEMON

Despite its small size, the book of Philemon is quite colossal, theologically speaking. It instructs us on forgiveness and does so in a unique and practical way. And while it does this, it gently teaches on matters of equality, fellowship, edification and more. Only 25 verses long, it packs 25 chapters worth of divine guidance for us all.

In this book, we will unpack these divinities so that we can think and behave more like our Lord, who is a forgiving God (Ex. 34:6-7). Technically, this book is called a "commentary" on Philemon; however, it has been written in a way that is unlike typical commentaries, which often read like textbooks, focus on individual passages, and have a choppy flow. The flow of this book is fluid, transitioning from point to point, like topical books do. However, in this book all of the points are posited by scripture. This is a commentary for those who don't like commentaries.

For more resources like this visit:

JacobAbshire.com